A Patchwork
of
Memories

Memoirs of a Decade

Stories about growing up in rural French Louisiana
in the 1950's

Written and Illustrated By
Yvonne Thibodeaux Bogan

Order this book online at www.trafford.com
or email orders@trafford.com

Most Trafford titles are also available at major online book retailers.

Note for Librarians: A cataloguing record for this book is available from Library
and Archives Canada at www.collectionscanada.ca/amicus/index-e.html

Printed in Victoria, BC, Canada.

ISBN: 978-1-4269-1715-8 (sc)

*Our mission is to efficiently provide the world's finest, most comprehensive book publishing
service, enabling every author to experience success. To find out how to publish your book, your
way, and have it available worldwide, visit us online at www.trafford.com*

Trafford rev. 9/25/2009

North America & international
toll-free: 1 888 232 4444 (USA & Canada)
phone: 250 383 6864 ♦ fax: 812 355 4082

Dedicated to the memory of my mom and dad

Eve and Clevens Thibodeaux
for their unconditional love and a lifetime of memories

We don't remember days, we remember moments.
-Cesare Pavese

O God of the past, present, and future, teach us to cherish our good memories, put the bad ones behind us, and look forward to future blessings from you.
-Laila Geitz

Foreword

People say memories fade with time, but that is not always the case. Sometimes memories become more vivid as we age and have time to reflect on our life experiences and all their meanings.

My memories came to me in "scraps" or "patches"-- the quilt patch, the peanut patch, the cotton patch, and all the other patches of my childhood. As I recalled and wrote about each memory or "patch" of my youth in the 1950's, I felt as though I were sewing my patches together, just as Mom used to sew her patches for a quilt top. My patches make up the first decade of my life, and like a quilt top each one has its own beauty and a story to tell.

The 1950's, a decade that was no easier or harder than any other, but maybe a little sweeter, safer and slower than the ensuing decades. By most accounts, a good decade.

My hope is that my memories will spark your own memories and emotions of your childhood. May you dwell only on the sweet ones.

Contents

When a Quilt Is
More Than a Quilt

I love quilts. I love the comfort, warmth, and the bright
and muted color patches that make up the quilt top. I also
like the weight of it as I lie underneath on cold icy nights.
I should say the weight of four or five quilts on cold icy
nights.

There's no heat in our old farmhouse, save the heat of a
small gas stove located in the living room. Definitely no help
in heating up the bedrooms. Really, unless I stand right in
front of the stove's brick burners, it offers little warmth. And
that's what I do to get my pajamas on for bedtime. I stand a
foot away from the stove, peel off my clothes, and, in a flash,
have my pj's and warm socks on, and race down the long,
dark hallway to my bedroom.

I hurriedly peel back the corners of one, two, three, four

quilts, then slide in between the double-layered, green plaid blanket. I curl up in a tight fetal position because the bed is like a sheet of ice. It's so cold and stiff, I swear, you could ice skate on it. The curled up position allows the body minimum contact with the icy blanket. Even my head is covered and it takes about thirty minutes to gradually thaw out. As I thaw, my legs and body gingerly stretch out under the quilts.

I say "gingerly" because the mountain of quilts is so heavy that it's like a bulldozing effort to ease out of the curl. There's no turning over in my sleep. It takes a conscious, Herculean effort to lift those coverings enough to roll over.

Quilting, for my mom and her friends, is for practical and functional reasons; it's not a hobby or a pastime. Our families need those quilts for survival in the winter.

There is room for creativity in quilt making in the form of stitching the quilt tops together. *The Wagon Wheel, Log Cabin, Star of David, Bow Tie* and dozens of other patterns can be coordinated in so many different colors, sizes and textures.

Some are stitched in solid fabrics only; some with mixed solid and patterned fabrics; some in bright, electric colors; and others in soft, muted colors of a flower garden. All are different, unique, pretty, and special.

Mom stitches her quilt tops on her foot-pedal Singer sewing machine. Patch after patch of scraps feeds through the Singer foot and ends up in one long row puddled in a heap on the kitchen floor. This row is now ready to be stitched to another one until finally the puzzle is complete.

It's now time to call a quilting bee together to assemble and hand-stitch the assorted components of the quilt. It's easy to get four or five neighborhood women together to quilt. All are eager to help because they know that the favor is returned in a heartbeat when they are in need. They also know it doesn't have to be a quilting need either. Any need will quickly bring family and friends to help. There is usually not even a chance to ask for help. The help arrives as soon as the need is known by at least one member of our farming community.

Quilting day arrives, and the ladies are here early in the morning. *Le café* is ready, but there's not too much time wasted on coffee. There's a quilt to be quilted with no time to spare.

The bottom fabric is laid down on the floor, and then the rolls of heavy, yellow cotton are placed on top with the colorful quilt top laid over all like the crown jewel that it is. The sides of the quilt are nailed to long, 1" x 1" boards to hold the quilt taut. Heavy twine, or *ficelle*, is tied around the four corners and looped through hooks in the ceiling. Now the quilt is suspended in midair in the center of our kitchen.

The ladies stake out their quilting space and pull up a

chair to the quilt. They get their needles, thread, scissors and thimbles and start stitching. In and out, in and out slide the needles. All is quiet while the ladies get their rhythm and stride going. In a few minutes the chatter begins in soft, soothing monotones with occasional laughter and girlish giggles. All of this is in French, of course. The rhythm of their words coordinates with the rhythm of their needles like a well- orchestrated dance, and the words and thread are both stitched into the very fabric of the quilt.

It's a comfortable, timeless, secure feeling of love and togetherness. I feel all of this emotionally in my young heart as I play underneath the quilt, which serves nicely as a tent, covered wagon, or any other place my imagination cares to take me.

It's no wonder I love quilts. They are a symbol of love, community, and security for me. They're beautiful and their creation represents hours and hours of patient hands gently and lovingly touching every square inch of fabric. Did I mention how warm they keep you on a cold winter night?

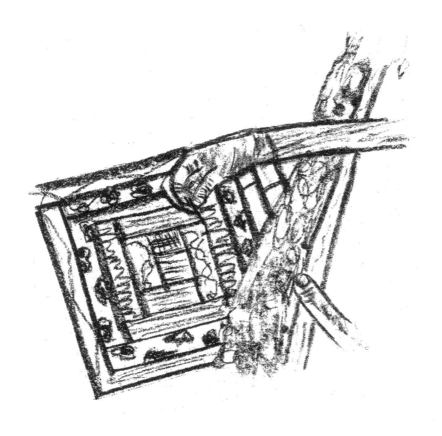

Cotton Pickin' Cotton

I know what it is to wake up early. It's been fifty years since I've heard my name being called to rise and shine, but I remember the feeling. Rise and shine at 5:30 a.m.? You've got to be kidding! Why, you may ask, would someone be yelling at me to wake up so early on a summer day when there's no school?

Cotton. That's right. We have to pick cotton. Our cotton, right across the cow pasture. Why so early? The grass, the plants, the air is so wet. Dew covers everything at this ungodly hour. But it will dry fast enough in the hot, scorching sun. Then you'll know why we start so early. It's the heat. It will claim you within a few hours. You will be begging for water and lifting your hat, hoping to get a tiny whiff of breeze against your wet sweaty hair.

Never mind that you wear loose, baggy pants, a long

sleeved white shirt, a big brimmed straw hat that ties under your chin; the heat and burn penetrate through it all. The long-sleeved white shirt is to reflect the sun; the long pants are to guard against insects and cotton boll scratches, and the hat is to shade your face from the sun.

But there's no thwarting the noon heat on a mid-July day in Southwest Louisiana. And there's no fooling yourself, either. It is hot! But the cotton is at its peak. Big and puffy cotton balls explode out of every boll on the plant. If it weren't for the heat, you could imagine what snow must look like after a fresh snowfall. (Not that I'd know what it looks like.) I'm seven years old, and I've never seen snow except in pictures when Mom read *Frosty the Snowman* to me.

On this day, we ride in the wagon with Dad driving the tractor, pulling us all along slowly through the cow pasture. We stop at the gate leading to the field where either my sister or I will jump down to unlatch the gate to drive through and then close and latch it back so the cows won't follow us to the cotton field.

We are all quiet, still in our own morning thoughts, finding our own cotton sack amid the heap of sacks in the wagon. Mine is easy to find. It's the smallest one specially tailored for me by Mom. Made of thick yellow cotton, it has a wide shoulder strap that fits over my head and on my shoulder. The sack is long enough to drag a foot or two on the ground; otherwise it would be too heavy to carry once I started filling it with cotton. This way I can drag it along the row and not carry the weight of it all day.

Dad pulls the tractor over to the patch where we'll be picking. We settle the water cooler under the wagon in the shade; otherwise we'll be drinking steaming water at noon even though the cooler is filled with ice.

Now there's no putting it off. We must start. I get to share a row with mom because my arms are not long enough to pick the opposite side of the plants. So I pull and stretch and bend and contort myself to reach as many bolls as I can. This is a two-handed job. My left and right hands pick simultaneously, and, when full, which takes only a few seconds, slide the cotton into the sack. My body's forward motion naturally shifts the cotton in the sack to the bottom. The rhythm of picking comes quickly--after ignoring the wet plants slapping at my body and my own hands slapping at the mosquitoes.

Soon I am lost in my thoughts again. Only an occasional slap or murmur is heard when someone either gets bitten by a mosquito or complains about the heat, the wet cotton, or the hunger. Yes, the breakfast we had an hour ago is quickly replaced with thoughts of lunch and water.

There are special calls for water breaks, usually determined by Dad. Of course, we have to be on the end of the row where the wagon is before we even hope for a water break. Usually, that's around 10 o'clock by sun watch. No one wears a watch to pick cotton, and time is pretty well measured by checking the position of the sun. I check it often. Not so much for the time but as an excuse to stand and stretch my back, and because it's hard for me to take this job as seriously as the rest of my family. Luckily, I'm given a lot of leeway due to my age and size.

Usually, after lunchtime, I'm excused from picking. I get to take a nap under the wagon. It's pleasant and private under there and offers a whole new world to me. It would actually be quite comfortable if it weren't for the ants. Regardless, I soon drift off to sleep and, low and behold, I dream of picking cotton and being bitten by ants.

Le Premier Jour D'École Blues

Or

First Day of School Blues

I am feeling anxious, a little nervous and uncertain of my future. I keep hearing talk of school starting in a few weeks. I hear things like, I am really *une grande fille* now and ready to start first grade. What in the heck are they talking about?

I know nothing about school. I know nothing about anything except my immediate home and surrounding neighborhood. Oh, I see the school often. After all, we pass in front of it several times a week. But in my eyes it is just a huge brick building with a flag flying in front of it. What can it possibly have to do with me?

Huge brick building? Now of course, a half century later, it seems so small when I go by. Just a small country school with lots of tall old fashion windows with an AC window unit sticking out from at least one classroom window. A modern update from my days, when the best we could do was to open wide all the windows and eat dust when the breeze blew. But the flag is still flying, and the circular drive is still in front, and the playground is still there, though now filled with playground equipment: climbing bars, swings, and tether balls. That's all new. Back then there is nothing on that playground but kids, a few balls and jump ropes and of course, jacks and pick-up sticks, the latter two always brought from home.

But I digress!

There is no way in my mind that I am ready to leave home, no matter what my mom and dad say, what my older sister says, or what the state of Louisiana mandates.

I have to form a plan of action. My first thought is to ignore it completely, and it will go away and never happen. Unfortunately, the school topic keeps coming up in conversations. My first plan is quickly defeated. On to Plan B! I plan to be so persuasive in my arguments that my parents will soon see the error of their intentions. So now whenever the topic comes up, I have my arguments ready. At five, I speak mostly French, and I am going to use that to my advantage!

"There's no way I can go to school," I say. "I won't understand a word the teacher is saying. You don't want the *maitresse d'école* to waste her time or mine. It's pointless!" Then, "Mom, you know you will miss me way too much. I've never been away from home. Mom, who will help you around the house with the wash and cleaning? You can't do it by yourself."

But all of these arguments fail. Mom always has an answer to each protest.

I feel my most legitimate excuse is the language one. After all, how am I going to learn if I can't understand the teacher? I use it ceaselessly, daily, that final week before school. All to no avail!

The dreaded day arrives. I am dressed in my new finery, one of mom's hand-sewn creations of course, to commemorate the day. Crying my heart out, I am put bodily in our 1955 Crown Victoria. They are really going to send me away and abandon me in that monstrosity of a building called school.

I am not defeated yet. I will fight this to the bitter end. If they can't get me out of the back seat, I won't be left there. My mother opens the back seat car door but I slide to the opposite side of the car seat, roll myself into a tight ball, and she can't reach me. Shutting the door she walks around the back of the car and opens the other door. But I am ahead of her and foil her attempt once again by sliding to the opposite side and doing my ball up thing. This is going to be easy, I think. Mom will tire out way before I will.

Oh, no! Now Dad gets involved. One parent at each back

door. What to do? Mom grabs me and I resist by kicking, screaming and yelling like a stuck pig. I am attracting quite a crowd by this time, but I am beyond caring. This is the end of my world as I know it.

Somehow, after a while, I am enticed to stay. But I am right. It is the end of my world as I know it in 1956. But it is the beginning of a better world for me and a multilingual one at that!

It's a Pig Race Out There

I grew up with the pigs. Well, what I mean is, there were always pigs in the pig pen on our small Acadian farm as far back as I can remember. I have a love-hate relationship with them.

I love watching their antics while they're eating or rolling around in the mud. They seem to live such a carefree life. It's like living in a pig amusement park. First of all, they have a huge L-shaped piece of prime real estate along the road side of our land. That's where one of the best climbing Chinaberry trees is located, smack-dab in the middle of their park. Tall, lush grass grows in the long leg of the L pen and under the tree. The short leg of the L is mostly hard, dried dirt or gooey, bubbly mud when it rains.

The fence where the feeding trough is located connects to the shed on one side and the barn on the other. It is an old board fence nailed to a couple of 2 X 4's but still sturdy enough to support my light weight as I sit on it for a front row view of their eating frenzy.

What a pig circus! "Souie, souie, souie" is the call to dinner. The second they hear the first souie, there is a mad dash to the trough. As the corn, mush and scraps are poured in the trough, it's like watching a wrestling match. I've never seen so much pushing, snorting, and oinking as each pig tries to get the biggest serving of the buffet.

Sitting on top of the fence or standing on the bottom board, I have a bird's eye view of the dinner scene. The pigs are entertaining to watch, and though rude and obnoxious to each other, all always seem to leave the trough satiated with food. They move much slower on the way out than on the way in to dinner.

The pigs are mostly different in dress and size, and I recall even naming a few of them based on their color or personality. Their daily wear consists mostly of black, white or spotted black and white. Though the colors may remind me of formal attire, I can vouch that they are very casual and mostly not too neat in appearance, especially after a rain.

I like watching them sleep, too. Seemingly oblivious to their surroundings, they stretch out on their sides with only a slight twitch to their eyelids, probably dreaming of the next bucket of pig slop.

I also hate these pigs. I have to warn you that their supine relaxed position is very misleading. I know from the number of times I judge them to be slumbering, only to be rudely chased by them in an amazing race of, "Take Her Down for Dinner."

You see, my goal is to make it to that big, lush tree right in the heart of Pigsville. It is the best climbing tree on the farm with a short, squat trunk and large, thick branches extending out from the entire circumference. A tree perfect for climbing, to read in or live out an amazing adventure of my choice. That tree offers so much fun and imaginative possibilities that I feel it is worth risking my young life to reach it. It also offers unlimited shade with its thick summer foliage and relief from the sweltering heat in the coolness of its branches.

I study every angle of my route to the tree based on the location of the pigs. I position myself on the top of the fence, slide off my flip flops for better traction, twitch my toes with anticipation, and take a few seconds to psych myself up for the sprint to the tree.

It is now or never. I jump. My first movement brings the pigs to their feet quicker than the jolt of an electric prod, but there's no turning back. I skirt large underbrush, jump over mud puddles, and fly like the wind with the pigs on my heels snorting and oinking their displeasure at my trespassing in their private resort. One final leap and I'm in the tree, thumbing my nose at the slain dragons underneath. I've lived my first tree adventure of the day. Now I'm free from danger for at least an hour in the strong arms of my fortress. I have not a care of how I am to make it back to the fence intact.

Pistache to Praliné

or

Peanut to Praline

I trek at least two steps behind Daddy's long strides trying my best to keep up with him. We walk down the well worn, slightly curved footpath through the pasture and on past the rows and rows of cotton, corn, and other farm crops and do not stop until we get to the back southwest corner of our farm. *Mais*, we must be walking all the way to China, I think.

Finally we arrive at our destination. The peanut patch. The peanut patch consists of two or possibly three long rows of peanuts planted about four or five months back. The peanut plant is short compared to the cotton plants and corn stalks neighboring it. Its foliage only reaches one to two feet up. But the best part of the peanut plant is not up but down underneath the ground where dozens of light brown shells are attached to the roots like barnacles on an underwater rock.

Dad grabs a stalk and pulls up the entire plant, including its roots with the peanuts attached. He picks off a few peanuts and cracks the shell open to see if the peanuts are ripe enough to harvest. Too green, or too small, he will wait a week or two before harvesting.

Close enough!" he exclaims, and he gives me a couple to sample.

We only eat a few because raw, unripe peanuts will knot your stomach up faster than small, hard, green apples. The next day we return to the peanut patch with the wagon and my mom and sister to pull up all the plants. As each one is uprooted, it is thrown onto the flatbed wagon. After about half a day's effort, we finish pulling up the plants but are not finished with the work.

Once home, Dad stows the wagon in a shed where we commence to pulling off the legumes and stashing them in large gunny sacks. We only fill the sacks about halfway so when laid out flat, the peanuts are single layered in the sacks. The opening of the sack is tied tight with twine, or *ficelle* (duct tape of the 1950's).

"What are we going to do with all the sacks of peanuts?"

I inquire, thinking this isn't conducive to eating peanuts, tied up in sacks as they are.

"They still have to dry out," Dad explains, as he steps out from the dark, musty shed to stare up at the sky. Not a cloud or a chance of rain in sight.

Dad promptly retrieves a ladder and starts laying out the sacks of peanuts on top of the shed's roof. There they stay for several days, ripening and drying out in the scorching Louisiana sun.

Over the next several days, I parrot frequently "Are they ready yet? Are they ready yet?"

I am old enough to remember from last year all the sumptuous treats those peanuts provided for us. Raw peanuts, roasted peanuts, both in the shell and shelled, and best of all, homemade peanut pralines. Sometimes Mom made the delicious candy with whole peanuts, and sometimes she made it with finely ground peanuts. Each kind has its own unique taste, each equally good in my mind. Both varieties are blue ribbon winners.

I can hardly wait for the freshly made pralines to cool off enough to eat. The chocolatey peanutty aroma wafts through the house. It takes all my will power, along with mom's admonitions, to keep me from eating them and burning my mouth.

Finally they are cool enough, and I let the first bite melt in my mouth as I enjoy the sweet buttery flavor on my tongue.

They are delicious! (My mouth salivates now as I recall the taste fifty years later).

Peanut work is tedious, and the wait before reaping its rewards is long--five to six months from seed to praline--but the payoff is exceptional!

Peanut Pralines

3 cups sugar

1 cup milk

1 tsp vanilla

1 tbsp. butter

2 cups ground peanuts (pecans may be substituted)

Mix sugar and milk and bring to a slow boil. Continue
to boil until it is at a soft ball stage then add vanilla and
butter. Add peanuts. Stir. Pour mixture in a buttered dish.
Let cool and cut into squares.

La Boucherie

The heat is finally breaking. Instead of a high of 100 degrees, it's probably in the low 80's. But by Deep South standards that's fall weather. After all, it is November and that means it's time for a *boucherie*. *Boucherie* is a French word meaning to butcher, such as a hog or cow, but that meaning is so limited. *Boucherie* to us Acadians is a routine fall tradition, if our family plans to eat meat in the coming year. It's a *coup de main*, a time of helping neighbors, an opportunity for camaraderie, but also a day of seriously hard work.

For the occasion, the chosen fattened pig is made ready to sacrifice its life for the sake of feeding the family. That pig elect is rounded out of the pig sty and let loose into the fenced-in barnyard. After all, no one wants to accidentally shoot the wrong pig. Oh no, not Betsy! I'm crushed. I've watched her grow from a newborn piglet to butcher big.

Betsy is the one that finally ignores my jaunts through the pigpen to get to my favorite climbing tree. She doesn't even bother chasing me anymore.

I've been hearing plans and talk of a *boucherie* for several days. I even witness the invitation to friends and neighbors for their assistance. But I really don't understand what all is involved. The word *boucherie* does not have such a gruesome tone to it. I certainly don't envision a gun, knife, or blood and guts when I hear it.

My family is up at 5:00 a.m. A huge, black cast iron pot is filled with water and set on a campfire to boil, which will take a couple of hours for that many gallons of water. A large barrel is set up in a shoveled out indentation in the dirt and positioned at a 30 degree angle almost parallel to the ground and close to the pot of boiling water. I think of the story, *The Three Little Pigs,* where at the end of the story the pigs have a big pot of boiling water in the fireplace ready to greet the wolf. I still don't have a clue of what is to come.

Friends and neighbors begin arriving around 6:30 a.m. During the greetings and hustle and bustle, someone gets a 22 rifle. I see him carrying it and walking into the barnyard with it on his shoulder. Like a light bulb, it dawns on me what is about to happen, and I'm frozen to the spot. Please don't shoot Betsy, I'm thinking. Betsy, by animal instinct, knows what is about to happen. She runs around wildly squealing, but there's no place to go but in a circle. As she runs to the bob wire fence where I'm standing, she looks at me with wild, wide eyes full of terror pleading for help. My heart is beating erratically and hurting like nothing I've experienced before. I run into the house and into my bedroom crying. The shot rings out, and I can't help but peek out the window to see the marksman walk over and stab the pig in the throat. From the wound, the men then bleed out the pig.

However sad and hurt I feel, I'm still fascinated with all the hoopla going on in the yard. I dry my eyes and venture back outside. Betsy is placed whole in the barrel which is now filled with the scalding water. She is twisted and turned in the barrel like a fair ride I saw at the Rice Festival once. She's pulled out and placed on a *traineau,* a sled-like cart on runners that you pull with a rope. The men commence to scrape off all the hair with long, well-sharpened knives. The head and feet are then cut off, the pig cut open in half, and the innards given to the women.

The women begin a disgusting job of squeezing out what seems like miles of intestines. The smell is awful. I am told they're cleaning them to use as casings for boudin and sausage. I wonder if I'll ever eat *boudin* or sausage again. Pan after pan of water is set out and those pig bowels are dipped and rinsed and turned inside out and cleaned some more. After each dipping, the water is left a little clearer.

These casings are stuffed with dressing and sausage mix already prepared by the women earlier, a recipe handed down through the generations of Acadians and stored in the memory banks of the women. (The recipe is probably an encoded DNA gene yet to be discovered, because I see no written recipe).

The women work quickly. There's still so much to do. Pigs feet to shave and clean for stewing or pickling, brain to be skillet-sautéed in pig lard. The tongue to be stuffed with garlic and onions and cooked in gravy, and backbone stew to be put to simmering. Uh-oh, I believe the latter two are going to be today's lunch!

The men are not loafing around either. They cut the quarters into portions to wrap and freeze, fill tubs with the pig fat, which will be used for lard, and fry cracklings in the big cast iron pot that's now half filled with hot lard.

I try to take in all the details as I run back and forth between the two groups. Surprisingly, nothing is really demanded of me except to haul cool water and stay out of trouble. That's easy when there's an experience of a lifetime going on all around me. I observe all the action and reflect on poor Betsy. I hope her siblings and friends are not in direct line of vision of this scene. But even if they can't see, I know in my heart they hear, they smell and they sense what is happening. (It's DNA encoded, just like those recipes).

Crossover

It promises to be another Sunday like most other Sundays in the year 1959. I am nine years old and certainly not anticipating any excitement or unusual events to occur on this most ordinary of days. We go to seven o'clock mass as usual, take off our "good clothes" and enjoy the visit from my older, married sister and her family. I can't believe she is the head of her own family now with a loving husband and two adorable tow-headed boys, ages four and three. It seems only yesterday that we celebrated her wedding. Luckily, they live only a few miles away, so she and her family often come to join us for the day on Sundays.

At this time, Mom is busy chopping vegetables for gumbo at the cooking area of our large country kitchen. My sister, Nanny--which is what I call her because she is my godmother--is standing at the familiar old farm table with her head and shoulders hunched over, leafing through a stack of magazines. She's probably searching for new recipes to try out on her family.

I am sitting in the sewing corner of our kitchen in a lightweight aluminum lawn chair, one of two brought in for extra seating. It faces a doorway leading to a long hallway which opens up into the living room. This chair certainly offers more interesting seating arrangements than our straight-back, cowhide chairs that I'm used to. I can perform all kinds of contortions in this chair and it stays upright. I swing one leg over the right armrest, then the other leg over the left armrest; I swing both legs over one side, then the other. Then the best trick of all, both legs swing over the back of the chair and my back and head rest on the seat. I get tired of not being noticed for my daring acrobatic feats and sit straight up and cross my long gangly legs in the seat, wondering if the outside activity might offer a little more excitement than what I'm experiencing in the kitchen.

That's when it happens. Just as quietly and lightly as you please, a young man, a teenager really, between 14 - 16 years old, materializes from the hallway into the doorway. He is wearing rolled up jeans, a short sleeved button-down shirt hanging loosely around his hips, and black and white high-top tennis shoes. He's tall, lean, and lightweight with dark hair. With twinkling eyes and a mischievous look on his face, he raises his index finger to his lips, as if to say, "shhh, don't tell. This is our secret."

My heart races. I'm perspiring and cold at the same time, and I feel frozen in place, like when we play freeze tag on the school ground. Through the other kitchen doorway leading to the living room, I have a clear view of the front door, the only way he could have gotten in, but that outside door is closed.

My mind races with thoughts of who this boy could be, how he got in, and what in heck does he want?

I am scared! I do not ever remember being this frightened before. In the short time it takes me to go into crisis mode, he slips behind the hallway door to hide. A good place to hide, I must say, since I have used it plenty of times myself. But we're not playing a game of hide-and-seek right now.

"Nanny," I whisper.

"Yea," she responds nonchalantly, clueless of the danger only a few yards from her.

"There's a boy hiding behind the hall door."

"What kind of boy?" she asks, not taking me seriously.

"Someone broke into the house. He's hiding behind that door," I say, jutting my chin out in the direction of the hallway.

She hears the tremor in my voice, takes one look at my face, and knows I'm not teasing. Cautiously, she turns toward the hallway and very slowly approaches the door. I can tell she is also a little frightened by now. She peeks behind the door.

"Nothing there," she proclaims.

"Then he must be hiding in the hall closet," I reply, positive that he is still lurking close by.

She checks all the hallway closets and the middle bedroom for good measure. Nothing! Nothing! Nothing!

"You're just imagining things," she says. "It's ok. There's no one in here," she assures me.

My mom and sister dismiss it as my imagination gone wild.

I'm still rooted to my lawn chair and positive it was not my imagination. I remember his mischievous grin and his fingers to his lips. Nothing moves except my eyes which continue to dart to all the visible door openings trying to figure out how he could have slipped away or catch him in the act of slipping out.

But slip away he did. And after about five or ten minutes, long enough for my heartbeat to slow down, I slip away too. I've had enough excitement in the house for a leisurely Sunday morning.

Many decades later, when I asked my mom and sister about that episode, neither had any memory of it. I however, have recollected that image many times over the ensuing years and have mused over who the mischievous boy could have been. Having had time to reflect on the incident, I now believe he was the spirit of my young brother who died at the age of four in 1945, five years before I was born. In 1959, he would have been fourteen years old. I think he decided to check-in on his family and dressed according to local fashion for the occasion. He may have even accidentally crossed over, not expecting a perceptive nine old sister to catch sight of him. But I'm sure we'll meet again later and laugh over the Sunday morning sitcom in the Thibodeaux household in 1959.

Sunday Dinner

Both my parents come from large families. Eight children on mom's side and ten children in dad's family. I am not short on aunts, uncles and cousins, but by the 1950's many of my parent's siblings have moved off the farms and into small surrounding towns or to *grand* Texas where the oil refineries padded their pockets much better than any farm work ever would.

Like in the classic children's fable, *The Country Mouse & The City Mouse*, I think that our family is considered to be the country mice, and my cousins and their families are the town mice. Regardless of our rodent class, it is always a treat to visit them in town, where there are sidewalks to walk on, next door neighbors, a nearby park and, best of all, an ice cream stand, where we can order soft serve ice cream cones for a nickel. And they, in turn, enjoy visiting at the farm, where we have chickens, pigs, cows, barns to play in, trees to climb and a *coulee* close by to explore.

Having no phone at our rural farmhouse, we are always surprised when the cousins decide to visit. I remember one of their rare visits on an early Sunday morning. I know it is early because we have just returned from Sunday mass, always an early affair, and mom hasn't started cooking dinner yet.

The debarkation from the two-door '52 Ford Fairlane reminds me of a circus act where many clowns plow out of a small boxlike cart. An infinite number of legs, arms and bodies climb out of the car. This is going to be a fun day, I think. I can tell from mom's expression she doesn't share my feelings. "What am I going to cook to feed this crew?" she is thinking. Of course, it would be unthinkable not to invite them to stay for dinner. But nothing has been taken out of the freezer for dinner, and there is no such thing as a nearby supermarket.

Not to worry. There's always fresh meat as close as our backyard. I know that one of the roosters is going to be done for! A handful of corn kernels is thrown out to attract the potential lunch. The hens and roosters circle around dad like a wagon train closing its ranks at the end of the day. Quick as a flash, Dad reaches down and grabs a rooster. It only takes another second to grab hold of the neck and give a mighty twist to the wrist to wring that rooster's neck. Lunch is thrown to the ground, but Mr. Rooster fights until its last breath. He flops and somersaults a few times around the yard, then expires.

A small foot tub of boiling water is brought to the back porch, and the rooster is held by its legs and dunked in the scalding water several times. It's easy plucking now as my cousins and I try pulling a few feathers off. Dad shoos us off and finishes plucking the bird in no time. He brings the rooster inside and singes it by holding it over the gas stove burner. This burns off the pin feathers and fuzz for a clean, minimalist look for our friend. *Pew yi*, the smell of that singed rooster stinks. The rooster is quickly cut up and thrown in the gumbo pot which is already boiling away with its roux-based liquid. Sausage links from the *boucherie* are also added. A big pot of rice is cooked and our dilemma of what to feed the city mice is solved. *Ma chère*, that is good gumbo. And talk about fresh!

Chicken and Sausage Gumbo

1½ cups lard	4 qt. water (cold)
Enough flour to make a roux	4 lb. chicken, cut up (rooster or hen)
(Approx. same amount flour as lard)	1 lb. smoked sausage
2 stalks celery, chopped	1 cup chopped parsley
	½ bunch green onions and tops
4 onions, chopped	

1 bell pepper, chopped

salt and pepper to taste

1. Brown chicken in some of fat in large iron pot. Remove chicken.

2. Add remainder of fat and flour stirring constantly until deep rich brown.

3. Add celery, onion and bell pepper.

4. Sauté all, stirring on occasion until it begins to separate.

5. Slowly add 4 quarts of cold water stirring constantly.

6   Bring water to rapid boil. Boil about 30 minutes. Then add chicken, allow to cook for 1 hour
simmering.

7. Add sausage, season to taste with salt and pepper. Simmer another 30 min.

8. When chicken is cooked, add parsley and fresh onion tops.

9. Serve over rice - sprinkle filé if desired.

The Old Farm Table

A friend recently asked me to accompany her on a mission to find the perfect dining room table for her small dining area. Together we visited an assortment of furniture stores, from high end price stores to flea markets, as well as antique markets. I oohed and aahed over all the beautiful styles: the currently popular pub tables and chairs that sit higher than the standard tables, rectangular tables, round and square tables, pedestal, draw leaf, drop leaf and every-leaf-in-between tables. There are a couple of dining sets that personally called my name, practically wrapped themselves around me and begged to be set free from their crowded, impersonal conditions and brought home with me. I envision each in my bay window breakfast area reflecting the morning sunlight from its surface as I sit enjoying my first cup of morning coffee.

There is only one problem. I already have a dining room

table, an old farm table, rectangular in shape and a perfect size for the designated area. Though not as attractive and eye-catching or even as practical as some I encountered, it does have strong sentimental value. There is no way I can part with it to make room for a new one.

My table is steeped with life's memories. They are written in hieroglyphics on every surface of the table. There's the indentation of the meat grinder where it is screwed onto the table top during a *boucherie* to grind meat or during peanut season to grind peanuts. There are tiny saw blade cuts on both edges of the long sides of the rectangular top. There's a hollowed out chunk where the hammer missed its mark. There are stains deeply embedded in the grain of the wood from blood, oil, and who knows what.

The farm table was the workhorse of our home. Though it measures only 34 inches by 48 inches, positioned as it was in the middle of the kitchen, it seemed in my youth to sit as big as our flatbed wagon. That table functioned for all our needs: it was a sawhorse for Dad's carpentry jobs, a cutting board for slicing meats, a sewing station for Mom to pin and cut out patterns for her many sewing projects, a work table for kneading dough for homemade bread, a counter for attaching the meat grinder, a work space for peeling and cutting fruits and vegetables for canning, a school station for me to do homework and study, and last but not least, a place for the family to gather for meals.

Life - so much life is embedded in this table. How can I get rid of it? There is no replacing timeless family imprints from decades of living. The table has a long family history. First it belonged to my aunt, mom's oldest sister. She and her family left their marks on it before it was passed on to Mom after her marriage to Dad. My siblings and I all grew up with that table, and it's as dear to all of us as we are to each other. Decades later, my nephew used the table and left his signature mark on it. He decided the table was too high for seating comfort and sawed two inches off the bottom of the legs. Later, he returned the table to mom and it was stored in the shed where it collected dust and cobwebs along with an assortment of odds and ends on top of it, until I rescued it in 1999.

That year my husband and I moved to a more spacious house and we needed a small table for the breakfast area. I showed the table to my husband on a visit to mom's, but I thought it was really dilapidated and in sad shape. My husband saw the potential in it and decided to tackle the restoration job. He sanded the entire table several times with a small hand sander. The surface just would not give up its stories no matter how much he sanded. The discolorations, indentations and imperfections stayed. I decided that I liked it that way. It's the Thibodeaux life line running through its surface like a vein of gold running through a gold mine.

My husband continued to work on the table. He primed

and painted the six inch skirting and the four round tapered legs white and he stained the surface, which is made from three one foot wide pine planks, a golden pecan color. We bought four slatted, ladder back chairs and stained them the same color as the table top. It's perfect, I think.

Today the table has even more scars. I use it as a drawing and painting table, library table and breakfast table. I've left permanent pencil and ink marks on it, tiny paint splatters that won't wash out, and my husband has added one inch round finials to the legs to bring the height back up. Nicks are on all the legs from pushing in chairs and hitting them with the vacuum or mop. I don't worry about the new scars - it's just another life line being stenciled in the table. Another decade and it will be considered an antique but it's the intrinsic value that stirs my soul. I wonder who will be next to inherit the table and leave their memories embedded in it? I hope they leave only good ones and cherish the old farm table as much as I do, in spite of all its flaws.

Polly Anna

When I reached the tender age of five, Polly Anna came into my life. She was beautiful, with long, curly, red hair; pretty, sky-blue eyes; porcelain-like complexion; and delicate splayed fingers on her tiny hands ready to extend a caress to your cheek. Her eyelids had real hair-like eyelashes on the tips and opened when you stood her up, then closed when you laid her down. She had moveable arms, knees that bent, and legs that walked when you helped her along. She may have been advertised as a doll when Mom ordered her from an ad in *Good Housekeeping* magazine, but to me she was my baby!

Santa supposedly left her under our Christmas tree that year, 1955. I had no inkling she had been patiently waiting in her box under the tree for my arms to gently lift her out of her imprisonment and then hug her against my scrawny chest. I had not asked for a doll or anything else for that matter.

With no television in the home, there were no commercials offering all assortments of toys, games, and other products. We had no newspaper ads or flyers or even catalogs peddling an endless line of toys. I probably didn't have a clue as to what to ask for on this very special day.

Our family has traditionally opened gifts on Christmas Eve. Surely, I must have had a couple of other presents under the tree when we opened gifts that magical night before Christmas, but if I did, I don't remember what they were. I'm sure they paled in comparison to my baby doll, Polly Anna. A unique name, you might think, for naming a doll, one a five-year-old probably wouldn't come up with. And you would be right. Polly Anna arrived with her own pedigree certificate and her own name printed in bold black letters on it. The name had just the right cadence and flair to it when spoken that it seemed perfectly suited to the doll's personality. She was and always has been Polly Anna or sometimes affectionately just Polly.

Polly was attired in a beautiful, silky, black and white plaid dress with white inlayed lace around the neck and around the sleeves and tiny red accent bows at the waist and in her hair. Her traveling ensemble included little white lace socks and white strapped rubber shoes on her feet. A black beret sat jauntily at an angle on her head giving her a very aristocratic look. Oh, *elle était belle!*

I played with her, walked along side of her and slept with her. Mom even sewed an entire new wardrobe for my baby. Beautiful little dresses and jackets that I could dress her in for our promenades around the yard.

Polly Anna and I were a happy twosome for many years. We had many memorable times together and celebrated dozens of holidays and special events with family and friends. She was loved and well taken care of until I finally outgrew playing with her. Even then she had a prominent position sitting on top of mom's *chifferobe,* like a lighthouse beacon, where she could observe much of our lives being played out and could still feel like part of the family.

Poor Polly. I cannot truly say I know how she met her demise. I remember seeing her on top of the old *chifferobe* even after mom left the farmhouse and moved into town. Years later, I spied her on a shelf in the spare bedroom closet. That is the last time I recalled seeing my dear friend. But the timeless cliché, that she didn't suffer and had a long and happy life, is especially applicable to Polly, I think.

I still love you Polly Anna, wherever you are. Thank you for enriching so many years of my childhood.

The Fork in the Road

It is an early summer morning. The sun is just presenting its first rays of light and casting its beautiful popsicle colors as a setting for our life stage. That stage being our small ten-acre farm in an area known in Cajun French as *la Pointe Noire*. *Pointe Noire* translates to the darkest point or black point, certainly an inappropriate name for our little corner of the world on this beautiful Louisiana morning.

My family, which today includes Dad, Mom, my sister and me, is walking single file down our much used footpath through the cow pasture. I am bringing up the rear as usual, stretching my spindly legs as far as feasible to keep up with the three adults. Even my sister, being twelve years older than I am, is an adult.

We are making our way to the cotton field on foot, not having the luxury of riding on the tractor or wagon this morning. They were left in the field at the end of the workday yesterday. Once the wagon starts filling up with our picked cotton, it stays in the field until time for the trip to the cotton gin.

About mid-way from the yard gate to the field gate, I see Mom bend over and pick up something with an expression of bewilderment.

"Mais, quoi c'est ça?" she asks as she ponders the object with an expression of puzzlement on her face.

She is holding a dirty plate and fork. Dirty, as in just recently eaten off of, with food just barely dried on it. We all gather around her to examine what seems to us an unusual archeological find. Questions are spilling out of all our mouths simultaneously.

"Who could have left this here?"

"Where does it come from?"

"Why is there a fork and plate on our path in the middle of our cow pasture?"

Who indeed would eat outdoors in the black of night on private land with real dinnerware, not paper or plastic mind you? That is the question of the decade. One we have no answers for, even though we all do a 360° survey of the area that resembles a rehearsed ballet pirouette hoping to spy the *who* in question. No one in sight. Is he or she hiding or sleeping in one of the sheds or barns or maybe hiding amidst the cotton or corn stalks? Are we being observed even now as we consider our rare find?

Dad decides we have spent enough time on a useless plate and fork and trudges onward toward the field. Mom decides she is not going to carry dirty dishes to the field and sets the dishes right back on the trail. And there they sat baking in the hot sun all day until they are picked up on our return walk home in the late evening.

When we arrive home Mom promptly throws the plate away in the outside galvanized trash can, but for some inexplicable reason decides the fork is worth keeping. It is sterilized and placed in the silverware drawer with all the other eating utensils. That fork, however, with its intricate engraved scrollwork stands out from all the other forks and never seems to fit in. I never select that particular fork for myself, and if I pick it up unintentionally, I make a deliberate effort to switch it out with another fork. Truly, I never observe the rest of the family eating with it either.

To this day, I've never forgotten that incident. I think the fork symbolized a family mystery and an invasion of our privacy that left us with an uncomfortable and vulnerable feeling. It was probably kept as a reminder that we are not always in control of things around us, no matter how secure we think we are, and it stands as a testimony to the many forks in the road we encounter in life. Or maybe, it was just a meaningless fork.

The Big Yellow Bus

What is it with kids these days? They do not want to ride the bus to school no matter their age. From the youngest kindergarten children to the highschoolers, they seem to be prejudiced against riding the bus. Where does this attitude come from? What seems like miles of vehicles stretch down several blocks in the close vicinity of practically every city school at both arrival and dismissal bells. They crawl forward a few feet at a time waiting to reach the school's driveway to pick up their little darlings.

That was certainly not the case in the 50's when I started attending school. There were no choices and no excuses. You rode the bus, except for the rare circumstance when a special need came up, and your parents picked you up.

Since I lived out in the country there was no possibility of walking to school. Early in the morning, with the mist and fog still hanging low, I had to begin watching for the bus. I'd jump up on the cabinet to perch and look out the window over the kitchen sink. From this vantage point I could see far down the country road and would watch and wait for the first speck of yellow to dot the road. I knew I had approximately five minutes from the time I sighted the speck to get my stuff, say my good-byes and be waiting on the side of the road, if I intended to make it to school that day.

The bus would turn at our corner and immediately had to brake to stop for me. Little sprays of gravel and dust would shoot out from under the wheels. I still remember the squeaking and swishing sound as the doors opened up to swallow me up inside the belly of the yellow beast. Mine was one of the first stops on the route, so all was still and quiet as I found my seat. Like at church, everyone pretty much sat in the same seat every day.

Whether the windows on the bus were down or up depended on the season, but it was always a difficult decision in deciding on the up or down position in the hot months. If they were up, it was stiflingly hot and unbearably smelly, especially on the ride home in the afternoons; but if they were down, we nearly suffocated with the dust blowing in like cirrus clouds all around us. The roads were all dirt and gravel, so there was no escaping the dust clouds that swirled in through the opened windows. Usually we compromised and left them halfway up. That way we could sweat and eat dust at the same time.

We'd rambled along mile after mile down the country roads,

making stop after stop until the bus seemed to rise and swell like Mom's homemade bread dough. The noise would swell too as farther along we went, due to the increased number of kids, but also due to the fact that we were finally waking up from our morning stupor. About an hour later, we finally arrived *à l'école*.

The trip home was almost identical to the morning ride but in reverse order. The noise level must have been at maximum decibel level for human ears at the onset of our journey but slowly dissipated as students were dropped off at their individual stops. The closer I got to home, the quieter it became because I, of course, was one of the last on the bus route to be dropped off. I was one of the first and one of the last each and every school day for seven years of my life.

I didn't seem to mind too much, or probably just didn't think about complaining, since I knew that was the way it had to be if I were to get an education. I forged longtime friendships on those bus rides. What a perfect time to whisper secrets head to head with friends, discuss the day's events, and share candy bars we hoarded all day especially for the long bus ride home. Those candy bars were extra scrumptious, because it took all our will power to refrain from eating them at school. Also, they were in that beginning melting stage, where they are soft and gooey and stick to the wrapper. We'd carefully peel the paper back and lick all the goo off the paper so as to not waste a single smear.

Sometimes we'd read our library books as we bounced along, and even with the words jumping all over the page, we were not daunted in our efforts to complete a chapter or two. Often, we'd start on homework assignments. I wonder if our teachers speculated at our unique squiggly handwriting from the bumpy bus rides. They probably thought it was a writing handicap inherited by all the children in our little farming community.

On more adventurous days, I'm sure we tested our lovable bus driver's patience. The boys were notorious for teasing the girls and being mischievous. Wadded up paper balls would sometimes fly across several seats to hit you on the back of the head. Jokes were told, pranks played, and tricks performed all for the sake of getting the girls' attention. Competition was fierce even at the elementary level.

Reflecting on that time, I understand how some would think riding the bus is so many endless hours of wasted time. But time is not wasted. It is filled with meaningful life experiences whether you are just sitting in your seat with your head bouncing against the window daydreaming of things to come, sealing friendships, sharing candy bars, or being teased. It's all good stuff that so many children today are not privileged to. So, parents, leave your car in the garage, save gas, and let your children ride the bus to school. They will make memories of a lifetime and as a bonus, maybe even do their homework.

Holy Week

Holy Week, the week before Easter Sunday, is a somber, spiritual sequence of days for all Catholics, but especially so for the Acadian Catholics of Southwest Louisiana. The French Acadians have a strong rooted religious heritage from hundreds of years of Catholicism. Religious holidays are honored and celebrated with fervor and reverence at each home throughout our community. It is an occasion for the family to attend mass together and spend the day together enjoying rituals handed down through the generations.

The week is honored with many church services beginning with the Blessing of the Palms on Palm Sunday, the Washing of the Feet ceremony on Holy Thursday and The Stations of the Cross processional on Good Friday. But the big *finale* is the celebration of the resurrection of our Lord on Easter Sunday.

These church rituals are important to our strong-faith Catholic community, but so are our home rituals in preparation for Easter Sunday. Easter eggs are dyed on Good Friday, since it is a memorial day of sorts, and no work or business can be conducted on that day. Eggs are plentiful around our house with all the laying chickens, and dozens of eggs are kept aside to be dyed for Easter.

I am astounded at the number of eggs boiled, each one to be repeatedly dipped in cups of colored water lined up on the old farm table like the colors of the rainbow. It is customary to dye one dozen eggs for each family member.

"Why so many eggs," you might ask. For pocking, of course.

Pocking is a unique Cajun tradition in which you compete with family and friends in breaking each others eggs. The word pock has been anglicized, but it originates from the French word *Pâques* which means Easter. It's a game where two people pair up and one person holds their hard-boiled colored egg in a semi-open fist position with the small end of the egg facing up. Your partner gently taps, taps, taps, on the egg with his egg until one of the eggs breaks. You listen intently to that small musical hollow tapping note until you hear and feel the defeating, cracking sensation of one of the eggs. You hope it is your opponent's egg. Each person quickly looks at his egg tip to check the results. The winner then challenges others to pock until someone ends up with a champion egg. A strong shelled egg will sometimes knock-out six or seven eggs from the competition. With large families, you can see why so many eggs are needed. Each person wants to pock with as many family members as possible. It's like the Easter substitute greeting. Instead of, "Good morning", it's "Let's pock!"

You can quickly go through a dozen eggs, but the large ends can always be used for pocking when all the small ends have been exhausted. It is a competitive and rambunctious egg game and you always have to be on the watch for the prankster who tries to slip in a guinea egg which has a harder shell than a chicken egg.

Eggs are recycled, though we didn't know that word in the 50's. A large portion of the eggs are made into deviled eggs as appetizers. Many are peeled and eaten immediately with a little salt and pepper sprinkled on them. Some are used for the potato salad, always on the Sunday dinner menu, and some held back for the after dinner Easter egg hunt.

Holy Saturday is baking day. Two or three cakes are baked on that day and set aside for Easter Sunday. I remember chocolate, carrot, and my personal favorite, coconut. The meals for the next day are planned and any meal preparations that can be done ahead of time are taken care of.

Easter is now just hours away. But it is not the religious ceremony, the Sunday dinner, the pocking of eggs, the Easter hunt or even the Easter basket that I look forward to. Though fun, they do not compare with the generated anticipation of wearing my new Easter clothes.

The excitement of wearing my new outfit is the greatest event of the spring season. Several times I sneak to the closet to try on my new white patent leather shoes. I walk up and down the hallway listening to the tiny metallic clicks they make on the wood floors. I have to be quiet, though my feet are eager to try a tap dance around the house in those shoes. But if mom hears me, she will yell at me to take those new shoes off before I scuff them up. It doesn't matter to me that they rub on my heels. They are new, beautiful and shiny enough to serve as a mirror. I can hardly wait to wear them with my new dress and hat.

This year, 1958, I wear a navy blue sailor dress with a gathered waist, a big white rectangular collar and matching white trim on the sleeves. There is also a long, four-inch wide, red tie that fits under the collar and ties in a big bow at the neck. My white, small brimmed, straw hat also has a white ribbon around the crown with the ribbon ends hanging down to my shoulders in back. Red bow in front and white ribbon in back. I look like a Christmas present ready to be unwrapped.

Finally the most special of days arrives, *Jour de* Pâques, Easter day.

The family attends early mass and returns home to wait for our company and begins preparing and cooking dinner.

For the Acadians, the noon meal is always called dinner and the evening meal supper. There is a meat dish; usually garlic-stuffed roast or baked ham or sometimes both depending on the number of guests coming. Rice dressing, of course, (no holiday or special dinner in a Cajun household can be celebrated without rice dressing), potato salad, coleslaw, homemade bread, deviled eggs and the *coup de grâce*, those many desserts.

We survive another family celebration with grace and merriment and manage to stay true to our traditions. My mom gets to demonstrate her excellent cooking prowess. Dad is declared winner of the pocking contest. My older siblings get caught up on family news. My brothers-in-law get to tell their exaggerated fishing stories. My nieces and nephews get to compete for the golden egg in the Easter egg hunt. And me, well I get to finally tap dance in those new shoes and wear my new outfit. All in all, a rather fulfilling and spiritual Easter Sunday. We have a lot to be thankful for, but I am most thankful for the big piece of leftover coconut cake. Hmmm, where can I hide that piece of cake?

Fast Pitch Softball

Tall, dark, and handsome. Every girl's description of the perfect man since Adam and Eve. I had that man in my life. He was my older brother. Thirteen years younger than he was, I can't say I spent a lot of time with him as a child. After all, what brother wanted a little squirt sister tagging along. But what time we shared was special.

My brother had a passion for softball. Not just any softball but fast pitch softball. He loved the game and perfected his underhand pitch well enough to be appointed pitcher of his team. The teams were made up of country neighborhood boys playing against one another. They had a coach, practice times, and a game schedule but no uniforms. It was all for fun, exercise and sport, but as with all team sports, it became serious and competitive.

I was so young at the height of his fame as a star pitcher,

only five years old, but I do remember attending one of his night games. My family seldom left the farm, much less the neighborhood, so an outing was always a special occasion. What made this one extra special was the fact that it was a night outing. The only place I ever went at night was either the back porch or, if in the mood for northern lights, the front porch. On that night, Dad, Mom my two sisters and I crammed into the Ford for the three mile trip to the softball field adjacent to the local elementary school. The road was dark, no such things as street lights back where we lived.

Could that be the reason it was known as *Pointe Noire,* the darkest point? On that particular night there were not even headlights on the curvy gravel road leading to the school. Occasionally we saw a soft, yellow glow in a window as we passed a neighbor's house on our route. It felt lonely and eerie to me but no one else seemed to be bothered by the lack of light. But wait, speaking of light, what was that I saw as we approached the playing field? Lights! Big bright, white outdoor spotlights. Wow, I was entranced! Was this Disneyland? A movie set? Heaven? No, it was the illumination of the local softball diamond, which I had never seen at night.

Many cars were already parked all around the perimeter of the softball field waiting for the start of the game. People were milling around, visiting, chewing, smoking, and eating. Some were still sitting in their cars with the car doors opened for a little air.

We found a parking space and pulled in facing the field and my two teenage sisters immediately jumped out to roam around. After all, what better place to catch some boy's eye? They were certainly plentiful that evening. I watched until I saw them meet up with friends and within seconds their whispers and giggles floated back to us on the night air and quickly dissipated in the white mist of the lights. Dad saw a neighbor he wanted to talk business with, an excuse for sneaking a smoke, as Mom and I both knew. I was allowed out of the car but had to remain in sight of Mom's watchful eye.

The mosquitoes were so vicious on that summer night; I periodically ran to the seclusion of the back seat of the car but found no relief there. No one got West Nile or any other deadly disease, but by the end of the evening we had lots of small swollen bumps and red welts from scratching them.

I really can't report to you any game stats, the score, or even if my brother's team won or lost the game. But I'll give them the benefit of the doubt and say they won the game. After all, they won the tournament that season.

What I do remember vividly are the bright lights, the mosquitoes, and the grand adventure of a night outing. And I remember my handsome brother, his cap on his head, holding a softball and winding up for his fast pitch. The spotlight shone on his face, and there was a definite gleam in his eyes and the look of stardom on his face.

It's All in the Thump

If you should ask what my favorite fruit is, I wouldn't have to think long. I'd say watermelon. I cannot resist that almost cotton candy texture of the sweet meat of the fruit. The way only the slightest pressure from the jaw squeezes out that sugary sweet juice and how it pools all around your tongue and mouth until you're forced to swallow. There is just no other taste that compares to this delectable fruit. My taste buds were sharpened and honed for sweets at the age of five by the majestic watermelon. I consider it majestic because of it size and beauty. It definitely would win the heavyweight championship belt if there were such a thing for fruits.

Some years Dad plants and cultivates watermelons on our farm. Oh, for that sweet July harvest! Just when the heat starts really cranking up in the South, the watermelons are ready for picking. We can hardly wait for that first watermelon of the season. Remember the peanut patch? Well now it is a watermelon patch. The back corner that was used for planting peanuts last year was deeply entrenched with watermelon seeds back in April, and we are about ready to eat the fruits of those seeds.

I walk with Dad to the outer corner of our world, past the rows of potatoes, beans, corn, and cotton and finally arrive at the watermelon rows. These rows are raised beds and much wider than the others because watermelon vines need plenty of room to spread out.

"Dad, how do you know if the watermelons are ripe?" I ask.

"Well let's listen," he replies. "Maybe they will talk to us."

Talking watermelons! I think dad has been in the sun too long. He then forms a small circle with his thumb and forefinger and gives the watermelon a good thump with the knuckle of his forefinger.

"Did you hear anything?" he asks.

"No, only your knuckle hitting the watermelon," I say.

"Good, that's what we want - a flat dead sound - not a hollow or ringing one. That means the watermelon is ripe enough to eat," he remarks.

I guess one ripeness test isn't enough for Dad because he performs another one. Just like school, I think, always one more test. He picks a melon up and turns it over to check its lighter underbelly. He examines the spot where it lay on the ground for a greenish yellow color, another sign of maturity and ripeness. The watermelons make the grade, but we won't know if it's an "A" until we cut one open.

Within a couple of days of the thumping tests, we haul the flatbed wagon to the watermelon patch and cut the melons off their vines and load them onto the wagon. Once home, the wagon is pulled into the same shed where the peanuts were stowed for a short time last year. The watermelons sit on the wagon in the dirt-floor shed. In here they will stay dry and somewhat cool.

I am excited about cutting the first watermelon of the season. And as a reward for our efforts, that's just what Dad decides to do. He perfects his thumping technique on several watermelons until he decides on just the right one. He carries it to the back porch where Mom already has the butcher knife handy. He sticks the long blade of the knife into one end of the melon. It cracks open on its own, a sweet one for sure. The melon is cut lengthwise along one of its green snake-like stripes. It splits in half and two deeply sunburned red faces with dark eyes and freckles look up at us. The halves are cut into slices and we each get one. We use no plates or trays but do use a serrated kitchen knife to cut out big rock size chunks. We sit on or stand around the back porch and enjoy.

The meat of the melon is still warm from sunbathing in

the field all day, but so sweet and tasty. The juice runs down my chin and down my arm all the way to my elbow before it finally plops in the dust at my feet. It dribbles on my shirt and on my legs where it leaves little washed out gullies of grime all the way to my ankles. The flies love all this sweet juice, and they too get in on the action. So there we are holding a chunk of watermelon in one hand, swatting flies with the other and spitting seeds out of our mouths. As you can tell, there's a fine art to eating back porch watermelons. Our spit out seeds make the chickens and the roosters really happy. They cock their little heads at us, and with their beady eyes blink their thanks at this unexpected treat as they cackle and flit all around the porch.

We continue to eat the entire watermelon, cutting the meat down to the white of the rind. The rinds are fed to the pigs. Nothing is ever wasted at our home. Everyone is in for a treat today. It is now time to average our watermelon grades. I give it an A+ for sweetness and it gets A's and B's from the rest of the family. It's an Honor Roll crop, that's for sure.

Cotton Princess

It promises to be another long, hot, humid July, not the kind of weather conducive to picking cotton, but, that's when it's in full bloom and ready for picking. We start picking around mid-July, and depending on the cotton crop and the number of pickers, we usually have a bale of cotton in five to seven days. In order to yield a bale of silk cotton, we have to pick 1500 pounds of raw cotton out of the field. The very best pickers, putting in a full day's work, can pick about 250 pounds on a good day.

After picking several rows of cotton, the sack finally reaches its capacity and everyone's sack is weighed on a cotton scale attached to a four-foot beam sticking out the back of the wagon. The scale is a long, iron bar inscribed with numbers. It has a hook for hanging the sack of cotton at one end and a bell-shaped, iron weight at the opposite end. At the end of the day, the workers are paid in cash, according to the number of pounds picked. Each evening, the number of pounds is totaled and logged in a small spiral notebook. That uncomplicated financial bookkeeping lets us know when we have reached 1500 pounds.

Cotton is puffy and balloons out like cotton candy. In order to pack more cotton in the wagon it has to be compressed. That is one of my jobs. I pull myself up the slatted sides of the wagon and tumble in. I jump, somersault, make cotton angels, and perform other assorted gymnastics to pack in the cotton. Though amusing, this is not as much fun as jumping on the bed because of all the seeds, leaves, and other field trash in it. It is also seasoned with little *chenilles,* (caterpillars) that burrow in the cotton and in my clothes. I am really good at flicking these off and consider it a game to see how far I can project one into outer space. I have the technique perfected; but then, I get a lot of practice.

The cotton has a strong, musty smell that lingers in the nostrils and on the clothes. This odor, along with the dried-sweat smell could be marketed as *eau de coton,* but I seriously doubt there is a big market for it. (Maybe now its time has come. I can see the ad, a macho man's aroma, a little musty with a hint of heat. A scent the ladies will not be able to resist).

After a week of fun jumps packing down the cotton, we finally have enough cotton to make a bale. It's time for the anticipated trip to the cotton gin. Dad hitches the wagon to the tractor, and we leave early in the morning to travel about a mile down the gravel road to the cotton gin. The cotton is picked, the workers paid, and it's now time for our reward. The tractor putts-putts down the road, pulling the wagon so slowly we don't even disturb the dust. If you look closely, you can see me sitting straight and tall in the center of the wagon, high up on the bale of cotton, like a cotton parade princess, practicing my smile and wave. I wave to the pigs, the cows, the neighbors, and an occasional car that passes by.

I've never been in a parade. Ever. Not as a child, a teenager or even as an adult. I've watched quite a few: Rice Festival parades, Buggy Festival parades, Mardi Gras parades and homecoming parades. I was always in awe and a little envious of the beautiful, poised girls standing on the floats or sitting on the hoods of the shiny, polished convertibles. Wearing their beautiful costumes, elegant, sequined gowns or current-fashion, homecoming suits, they were every young girl's vision of what a princess must look like. The closest I've come to being in a parade was my trip to the cotton gin. Yes, the cotton gin trip was a simulated parade of sorts for me; I felt as much a princess as the ones in the real parades.

At the cotton gin we pull up in line with all the other farmers to get a ticket, kind of like at the Department of Motor Vehicles, only this is Department of Cotton Wagons. Some wagons are pulled by mules. They are fascinating to watch from a distance. I don't dare get too close. The men catch up on news, discuss the weather--of paramount importance to a farmer--and talk about the price of cotton. I get a greeting of, *"Comment Ça va, 'tite fille,"* (how are you little girl) and a pat on the head. I'm more of a novelty than the mules.

After several hours, we pull the wagon up to the big, cylinder chute protruding from the side of the cotton gin. Like a huge, galvanized straw, it fits over the cotton and sucks it up, where it vanishes in the belly of the cotton gin. When I next see the cotton, seeds and trash have somehow been removed from it, and there it sits: a beautiful 500 pound bale of pure cotton. It feels so fine, soft and silky, unlike the cloak of burlap strapped around it to contain it in a bundle. Dad is paid for the total number of pounds brought in and on the quality of the processed cotton. I don't know what dollar amount that calculated to, not much in that era, but there's enough for me to buy a candy bar from the little store next door. I eat it on the trip home, this time sitting up on the tractor with Dad. It still leaves me a free hand to perfect my wave. You never know when you might be invited to be in a real parade.

Homemade Ice Cream

Today we are bombarded with a great quantity and assortment of sweets available in every supermarket, convenience store, movie theater, and just about every place you enter. We are a population addicted to sugar and our addiction is being fed at every turn.

In my childhood, treats were not so readily available. Sure the country stores and supermarkets sold a wide selection of sugary products, but how often did we go to the supermarket? Maybe once or twice a month. Plus, the trip to the store didn't necessarily guarantee a candy bar. I just used positive thinking and imagery on the entire fifteen mile trip to town. (I intrinsically knew *The Secret,* way before that book was ever published).

To satisfy our sweet tooth back on the farm, we ate fruit. We had three orange trees, a kumquat tree, and watermelons in the summer. We would also barter with our neighbors who grew pears or figs. And we had peanuts--though not a fruit--it definitely provided a satisfying taste for our cravings.

But the best and most anticipated treat was homemade ice cream in the scorching summer months. Mom and Dad would invite friends and neighbors over for this irresistible, refreshing treat, usually on a Friday evening in celebration of completing another hard week's work. It wasn't only the delectable taste we looked forward to, but the actual process of making our own ice cream. The anticipation began to mount as soon as Dad retrieved the ice cream freezer from the *cabane,* (the shed).

The outer shell of the freezer was constructed of two inch strips of cypress beveled on the edges to fit tightly together in a circle measuring about twelve to fourteen inches across. Three metal straps encircled the bucket at the top, middle, and bottom to secure it. Inside the outer bucket was an aluminum cylinder with two wooden paddles made with small wooden strips resembling dollhouse size window shutters. I recall some kind of metal gear top with a Z shape handle connected to it. This lid snapped over both bucket and cylinder and locked everything in place.

While the men took a ride to the nearby country store to purchase a solid block of ice, Mom and the ladies were in the kitchen mixing up the eggs, sugar, milk and vanilla mixture for the ice cream. The men returned home with the ice block and the entire company retired to the backyard, sat on the edge of the porch, the porch steps, or in cowhide chairs and commented on the general well-being of the chickens. They were anticipating something too, though they didn't know exactly what.

The men chipped the 25 pound block of ice and layered ice and rock salt in the space between the outer bucket and inner cylinder of the ice cream freezer until it was filled. The ice cream mixture was poured into the aluminum cylinder, and the turning mechanism was secured on top ready for someone to turn the handle. Several towels were folded and placed on top of the freezer as padding to sit on. A job just right for my size. I sat on the towels and my legs were just long enough to plant my feet firmly on the ground. It was a cool seat--literally--not as exciting as the throne on top of the cotton wagon, but still nice. As my weight steadied the freezer, several people took turns turning the handle at a slow and steady pace.

After about twenty minutes or so, it became really difficult to turn that handle, and the person cranking had to put all his weight and muscle into it. That was when you knew it was ice cream; the handle would no longer turn, no matter how much force you exerted. We then had to wait five or ten minutes to let the ice cream firm up. Ten minutes that felt like an hour to me.

Mom went into the house and came out with a tray

stacked with bowls and spoons. The ice cream was dished out, bowls passed around, and for a few minutes all you heard was the clinking of spoons on bowls and sounds of culinary pleasures like mmmm, *Ça ce bon* and *magnifique.* The chickens chimed in with their cackling and scratching seeming to say, "Where's our treat?"

We finished off the ice cream, rinsed out the buckets, and remained seated outside enjoying the colors of the sunset. They slowly turned from red to violet to magenta and finally faded into black. There was small talk until the mosquitoes became unbearable. Night was now upon us and our company said their thanks and goodbyes and departed for home. We washed the ice cream dishes and murmured our praise again for the delicious treat and our thanks for our friends. All in all, a very relaxing way to spend a summer Friday evening in *la paroisse Acadie.*

The Old Shaving Mug

I have an old shaving mug stand. It's the kind that has a hinged lid that lifts up with a mirror on its underside and a small white glass bowl that holds the cake of shaving soap. Along side the soap cup there are two small metal prongs to hold the shaving brush, although the brush is long gone. It's quite a unique item in 2007, but was a very common shaving necessity before and during the 50's.

I discovered the shaving mug about fifteen years ago in Mom's shed. It was hiding amid old jars and pottery. Its color was completely obliterated and its metal edges rusted, but the soap cup itself was not chipped or cracked. I found it a charming little piece and recognized it immediately as Dad's old shaving mug and brush holder.

I took it and several other old relics from the past, an old galvanized gasoline can with handle and spout, old pottery bowls and two heavy cast black irons, into the house to ask mom if she would be willing to part with them. She said I could have them since they had been sitting in the shed for the last twenty-five years. She wasn't planning on using them again.

I was especially attracted to the shaving mug and was taken back in time as a small girl when I would watch Daddy shaving. I remembered he kept the mug stand in the medicine cabinet over the bathroom sink. Along side the sink was a long, brown, three-inch-wide leather strap hanging ominously on a nail. I was told a horrid story of what that strap was sometimes used for; however, I never witnessed it being used for anything other than what it was intended.

Dad would take out an amber handle, straight-edge razor along with the mug in preparation for a shave. He would open the blade edge of the razor and strop it back and forth on that strap to sharpen the blade. The sink was plugged up and water put into it to clean out the soap from the soap brush. Amazingly, he would often shave with cold water, since we didn't have a hot water tank for heating water. He would wet the brush and swish it circularly on the cake of soap until there was a good rich lather, then brush a thick lather on his face. He would stretch his neck up with his chin jutted out and pull that straight blade up the side of his neck. Scritch, scritch, scritch was heard as he repeated the process up the other side of the neck and over the Adam's apple. He finished the neck and hurriedly scraped his face free of whiskers. This was after all a workday, not a special occasion, and this shaving business was not worthy of taking up too much of his time. He rinsed out the sink, brush and razor and put everything away. He was ready for another day on the farm.

I took my treasures home and washed, restored and displayed them around the house. Today, the shaving mug sits in my bathroom with a small candle in the soap dish. It's a tangible gift from the past that offers sweet scents and sweet memories of a bygone era, and of a very special person in my life.

Une Traiteuse

In the 1950's, it was much less common for people to see a doctor for an ailment than it is today. There were many and varied reasons for not seeing a physician: the distance to town, the lack of a driver in the family to make the trip to town, no medical insurance, no income for doctor's bills, a generalized belief that time would heal most ailments, and the availability of the healing ways of the local *traiteurs*.

A traiteur, treater of ailments, could be of either gender, would be of mature age, and usually specialized in only one or two areas, very much like your specialized physicians of today. One might treat for sunstroke, another for warts or infections, and another for earaches. Occasionally, a *traiteur* had the gift that enabled him or her to treat for an assortment of ills.

The gift of being a *traiteur* was handed down through

the generations. A woman handed it down to a younger man and a man to a younger woman. The special prayers accompanying the treatment were kept secret until the time to transfer the calling to the next generation. There were other rituals associated with the process, such as, the patient was not allowed to give payment, or even say thanks after a treatment.

Traiteurs took their healing gifts seriously. They were not voodoo people or witch doctors, but church parishioners with a strong faith in God, who believed they could help take someone's pain away by interceding to God on behalf of the patient. They gave all glory to God for any healing; therefore, did not accept payment or thanks.

My mom was a *traiteuse* of sunstroke, a very common and prevalent malady of the farm workers back then. With the hardest farm work occurring in the long, hot, days of summer, many people were stricken by sunstroke. Friends of friends, or even complete strangers, sometimes knocked at our front door, asked if Madame Thibodeaux lived here, and if she treated for sunstroke. Word of mouth was the only advertisement for a *traiteuse*. I never witnessed Mom refusing treatment to anyone that approached her for help.

She invited the person into the kitchen, or sometimes would bring a chair out to the shade of the front porch. She would wash her hands thoroughly like a surgeon prepping for the operating room. A hand basin of cool water was brought out and set on the kitchen table. I remember her hands dipping into the basin and then lifting up out of the water, where she then gave them a slight shake over the basin. She laid her left hand on the ailing person's forehead and her right one on the back of the head and slid her hands up the head. The process was then repeated on the sides of the head. It was always an upward motion, like she was drawing out the heat and pain from the top of the head. Her mouth was moving in softly murmured prayers as she performed her ritual, the prayers not loud or distinct enough to be understood. She then dipped her hands in the basin again, and dried them off on a clean towel. The same procedure was repeated twice more, at fifteen minute intervals.

I can't say that everyone who came to the door was relieved of their pain, but in many cases Mom got word that the patient felt better by the evening or the following morning. I do recall a couple of patients that were amazed at the instantaneous healing. They arrived in great distress and left talking and laughing and had great difficulty suppressing their thanks and appreciation.

As the years and decades went by, there was less need for a *traiteuse*. Air conditioners came into existence and people stayed in the comfort of their cooled homes and out of the hot sun. Even farm equipment, tractors, combines and cotton pickers were eventually air conditioned and were doing the heavy farm work of the laborer. More people were getting medical insurance and going to the doctors for their care. Modern times looked askance at *traiteurs* and saw their treatments as silly, superstitious, or on the dark side.

I believe Mom's last treatment was sometimes in the 1960's, except for the one time I asked for a treatment in the mid '80's. And, yes it did help. I don't know if it was the treatment itself, Mom's loving cool hands on my face and head or a transpiring placebo effect. The reason doesn't make any difference to me. What matters is that the pain went away. And no, she never did pass her gift on before her death in 2001.

One Saucer, No Cup

I had a very professional statuesque fourth grade teacher. She was always beautifully dressed with matching coordinates, had perfectly coiffed hair, wore big, flashy jewelry and spiked heels every single school day. Her name, appropriately so, coordinated with her looks, Mrs. Whip.

Mrs. Whip commanded the respect of her class, not only with her looks and name, but with her management style. She was organized, stern, and a strict disciplinarian, but also a loving and caring teacher.

One day Mrs. Whip announced that we were going to do a science experiment related to growing crystals, and each one of us needed to bring a saucer from home.

Now by fourth grade, I had very good command of English but was still limited in my vocabulary. I had no idea what a saucer was and had never heard the word before.

Obviously, Mom was not acquainted with the word either because when I explained to her I needed to bring a saucer to class, she told me she couldn't give me something if she didn't know what it was.

The following day our teacher read off a list of names of students who had not brought in a saucer. Of course, my name was on it.

After school, I again informed Mom about my saucer dilemma, but she had not received any clarification on the subject and couldn't help me out.

A few days later, the saucerless list presented itself again--only now it was a list of one--Yvonne Thibodeaux. For some reason, I could not bring myself to ask what a saucer was or to tell my teacher I did not know that word. Surely, I was supposed to know it, everyone else in class had obviously known what she was asking for.

Mrs. Whip walked to the back of the room, grabbed one of the saucers off the shelf and waved it at me.

"You bring your saucer in tomorrow," she said. "Last chance."

Une soucoupe, aaah, the light bulb came on for me. She wanted a *soucoupe!* We had plenty of those at home. I just nodded my head yes; I would have it by tomorrow.

I got off the bus and ran into the house with my new word spewing out of my mouth. I pulled myself up on the cabinet and opened the door where Mom kept the cups and saucers. I waved a saucer in Mom's face.

"This is what my teacher wants," I exclaimed proudly, having finally figured out the puzzle. "This is a saucer!"

Mom was still a little hesitant about giving up one of her saucers. I knew she was wondering if she would ever see it again, and I didn't have an answer for her. Solving the saucer mystery was satisfying enough for me for one day's work. She couldn't expect me to have all the answers. She looked over her stack of saucers and handed me the oldest one with a chipped edge. Good enough, I thought. Mrs. Whip could scratch my name off her list.

It was fitting that many decades later I would be the teacher in a classroom of limited and non-English-speaking children, children who often stared at me with a look of bewilderment on their little faces. Their faces showed they were so eager to please, but they still had not unlocked the mystery of the English words. I never forgot my fourth grade saucer experience and used that memory to help my students expand their English vocabulary. I kept an abundance of pictures and actual items in the classroom to show them, so they could associate the word with the object. I dramatized, drew stick figures, pantomimed, and flashed pictures-- everything but stand on my head. It worked! Children are such sponges when it comes to absorbing a new language or any knowledge, for that matter.

Mom did eventually get her saucer back, but she really hadn't missed it. Even if the saucer had never been returned, it was a small price to pay for the acquisition of our new word.

The Great Mouse Hunter

It's in the wee hours of the morning. I'm in that deep sleep when one supposedly gets her best rest. Mom is shaking my shoulder and telling me she needs my help and wants me to get up. Help with what, I think. It is 2 a.m.! I stretch my eyebrows up trying to get my eyelids to open. I only manage a slit, close them again and burrow even deeper under the quilts.

Mom tries again to wake me up. I can tell from her voice she is frustrated, and a little bit angry. I didn't do anything, I think. She tells me that for the past three nights a mouse in her bedroom has been keeping her awake. It squeaks, scritches, and even thumbs its little nose at her. She is ready for battle and needs my help.

I know we have a mouse problem at home. Fields of grain and vegetation surround our house, a perfect haven for rodents. Why can't they be satisfied with the great outdoors? Why do they have to intrude on our space? However, they tend to do just that, especially during a drought or in the winter.

We set mouse traps loaded with cheese or peanuts. We try to vary their menu to entice them to the banquet, but they are little Houdinis, these mice! We sometimes hear the trap spring, but there is no mouse in the trap. However, they do manage to steal the appetizer. I think the traps only encourage them to come into the house. They spread the word of free food to their family and friends, and pretty soon we're running a peanut kitchen for mice.

Mom's mind is set. The bedroom mouse has got to go. Tonight! Now!

I reluctantly get up, only semi-listening to her battle plan. What she has in mind is definitely a two person job. I protest her strategy, but like a general of a great army, she is on a mission, determined to win this battle.

We collect our ammunition. A broom and two old hard-sole shoes. We barricade ourselves in the bunker, her bedroom. We strategize our positions, me at the closed door, and she with the broom in hand, on all fours at the bed. The chase is on.

I can tell this is not going to be a quick battle. Mom's room is packed with cartons and boxes of quilt scraps, outgrown clothes and who knows what. The boxes are under the *chifferobe*, under the bed, and stacked up by the door. A thousand places for a little mouse to hide. I already sense defeat for us!

She begins by sliding out some boxes and poking around under the bed with the broom. I crouch at the door with a shoe in one hand already looking worn and battle-fatigued. I pray that tomorrow none of my friends ask me what I did the night before.

After a couple of minutes of shoving boxes and poking around--success-- a mouse runs out. This mouse is so fast; it's like a little gray streak of lightning. I do the late night shuffle and start slapping the floor with my shoe. I miss! Round one goes to Flash-Lightning. However, guarding the door as I was, he is still contained on the battlefield. Mom regroups and starts her attack under the *chifferobe* where Flash disappeared. Again, his hiding place is jeopardized; he's on the run. Only now, he has a buddy with him. Not one, but two mice, and they are not blind! No wonder Mom was kept awake. Mom slams the broom on one, and I do my shoe slapping thing. Bam, bam, bam, bam, bam! The sound ricochets off the walls like a fully-automatic rifle being fired. My strategy is simple. If I fire enough ammunition, I'll eventually hit something. It works! I feel the lump under the shoe. I whack again, and then again, to make sure he doesn't revive.

Two conquests, not one, but two! Mom has a look of

victory on her face. My look is only one of sleepiness and disbelief that I am a great mouse hunter in my own house.

The mice are disposed of, and I silently pray that the rest of their clan will get the message loud and clear. NO MICE ALLOWED! Mom puts her room back in order, and I slip back into bed. What feels like only five minutes later, I feel Mom shaking my shoulder and saying, "wake-up, wake- up, it's time for school."

Thou Shalt Not Steal

Morality never hung heavily on my mind as a child. By age six, I had no recollection of having to learn lessons the hard way: by the rod, razor strap, tree switch or even angry words. Probably that was due to my patient, even-tempered parents and not any saintly living on my part. Also, the church teachings were a huge part of our lives, and both my parents were always excellent role models of good clean living. The isolated, simple farm life I led did not frequently offer any true test of my faith and morality.

That was, until I started first grade in 1956. At that time, I was introduced to new temperaments, personalities, and temptations. One of my country cousins, on Mom's side of the family, was also starting first grade. We knew each other fairly well previous to the start of school, and she sat two rows over from me in class.

One morning she came into class with a fistful of brand-new, yellow number 2's. Oh, those were so beautiful! There was nothing like a long, new, sharpened pencil with a full head of eraser on it. All my pencils were short stubs, with chewed up aluminum tips, where I attempted to squeeze out one more erasure from them.

Her first act of the morning was to march right over to my desk and show off her new acquisitions. I will not lie. I was envious, jealous, and I coveted those pencils. I asked the appropriate questions: where had she gotten them, who had bought them for her and how many did she have? I commented on the fact that she certainly had a lot of them and even asked what she planned on doing with so many pencils? She mumbled some replies, but didn't seem to have any desire to share her bounty.

That morning, until first recess bell, I kept glancing over at her desk. I could see where she had stashed her treasures, all loose and easy like, among her books. I don't recall formulating a plan to acquire a pencil from her, but like the excuses given by many convicted felons, the opportunity just presented itself without premeditation.

I lagged behind at bell time and was last in line to file out the door. As I went by her desk, I calmly reached down and grabbed a pencil. I walked over to my desk and slipped it inside, before continuing outside to the courtyard.

I didn't say anything about the pencil until that evening

at home, when I was doing my homework. I couldn't resist showing my beautiful new pencil to Mom. I didn't realize she would be so inquisitive about it. I just wanted her to admire it, that's all.

"Where did the pencil come from?"

"School."

"Who gave it to you?"

"My cousin."

"Why would she give you a pencil?"

"Well, she didn't exactly give it to me," I began, and the whole story came out.

Mom in traditional fashion did not scold or yell; just sat me down and explained the eighth commandment to me. Stealing was bad; what I had done was wrong. The most difficult part of the lesson was being told I had to return the pencil the following morning and had to apologize for taking it.

"You are never to take anything that doesn't belong to you," she added vehemently. End of lesson, I thought.

The next morning I did as I had been told. My cousin just looked at me stone-faced, and without a comment took her pencil back.

A few days later, Dad invited me to go with him to visit a neighbor he needed to discuss business with. I went for the ride, where I was pampered and coddled by the Mrs. and her high-school-age daughter. They invited me inside the house while the men stayed outside to talk. I was offered milk and cookies, which I accepted. A bag full of costume jewelry was then brought out for my inspection. All sorts of baubles and beads, that they apparently wanted to get rid of, were offered to me. My eyes bulged and I got an excited feeling in my stomach about all that shiny fun stuff. I ran my hands through the treasure and caressed each piece.

I politely shook my head and said, "No, thank you."

They both looked at me in disbelief! What little girl doesn't like jewelry! They repeatedly made the offer, but I held firm with Mom's words ringing in my ears,

"Do not ever take anything that doesn't belong to you."

Later, back at home, I told Mom how righteous I had been about the bag of jewelry. What! She couldn't believe I had not accepted their gift. I was definitely confused! I reminded her of what she had told me only a few days before. She again sat me down and this time informed me of Part B to her statement. Don't take anything that isn't yours; but when it is offered to you as a gift, graciously accept with a smile and thank you. Now she tells me! Too late, I think. I hope Mom has learned her lesson; do not teach a moral only half way to a six year old. They take every word literally.

Irresistible Piglets

Spring was always interesting on the farm. I witnessed all the new plant growth in the garden and fields surrounding us and the birth of new animal babies: calves, chicks and my favorite, piglets.

One of the sows would find a deep, dark corner of the barn, lie in a bed of straw, and proceed to deliver anywhere from six to ten baby pigs. Granted, the first few days the piglets were not very attractive. They looked like oversized rats, but after a few weeks, they were irresistible. They had new, pink, baby skin, big dark eyes with down-curled eyelashes, little triangular ears, and a little loopy tail that looked like it had been set in a pin curl overnight. *Chère* little things, I thought, and couldn't help but pick one up. Their little, smiley snouts twitched, and they squirmed a bit, but like a fussy baby, they soon settled down in my arms.

As a young farm girl, I could not resist the little darlings. They were the perfect weight and size for a real baby feel. However, as they got bigger, they no longer wanted to be held, and in order to hold one I had to chase them around the barnyard. Once caught, I would attempt to wrap a blanket around it as you would a baby. This is not an easy task for a little girl and a squirmy pig.

Dad finally intervened on behalf of the pigs. I was instructed not to chase the piglets; they were not dolls to play with, they could get hurt jumping out of my arms, or I could get hurt by the sow protecting her offspring.

I heard and understood the new rule, and the pigs were free of me for a few days. Then one afternoon, while I was sitting on my tree swing, the sow and her brood were milling around under the tree, almost in arm's reach, practically begging to be picked up. I forgot all about Dad's warning. I jumped out of the swing and the chase was on. Unfortunately, Dad was nearby and caught me in the act.

That is the only time in my life that I remember learning a lesson by corporal punishment. Today, I don't know if the memory is more a trauma because of the spanking, or a drama because of the loss of my babies.

Courir de Mardi Gras

There's Something in My Attic, There's a Nightmare in my Closet, There Are Monsters Everywhere are all popular children's books enjoyed by today's youngest generation. I wasn't exposed to monster books or scary stories as a child. I didn't need them. I had the real monster deal, *le Courir de Mardi Gras!*

On a cool, February day in 1957, at the age of six, I experienced my first *Mardi Gras.* From inside the house, I heard whooping and hollering in our yard, so I stepped out on the front porch to investigate. There I encountered my first monsters! Never had I expected a scene right out of a horror movie in our front yard. In our driveway was an opened trailer being pulled by an old truck. In the trailer, were what I considered aliens, though I soon realized they had to be humans, since they walked upright and were talking and singing. But what kind of humans were they?

They were all dressed in outlandish, brightly-colored rags, worn in a layered look. Their faces were hidden behind finely meshed screen masks that had weird facial features painted on them. Fringed, cone-shaped hats perched on some of the heads. Some of these people were in the wagon, and some were chanting, begging, and dancing around the yard.

I'm not sure what I would have done had my dad not been standing out there among them. At first, I was afraid for his safety in the midst of this band of wild creatures, but if he was frightened, he was putting on a brave front. In fact, the creatures appeared to be begging and coaxing Dad for something. I made out the words *une poule* and *cinq sous*.

"Why do they want a chicken and a nickel?" I asked myself.

Dad called and waved me over to him, but there was no way I was going any closer to those heathens than I already was. He then threw nickels out in the yard and in the wagon and they commenced to more yelling and shenanigans as they competed to catch the coins. The money seemed to appease them; they all got back into the wagon, left the driveway, and headed down the road to the neighboring farmhouse.

I stood frozen in stunned astonishment from the safety of the porch.

"What was that?" I called out.

Dad explained that they were only neighbors dressed in costumes and wearing masks. They meant no harm.

"Did you give them nickels so they would leave?" I asked.

"No," said Dad, "I gave them money to help pay for the big gumbo they are planning to cook at the church hall tonight. They are collecting ingredients for the gumbo: chickens, sausage, onions, as well as money to help pay for the stuff they don't get on the *Courir de Mardi Gras*."

Dad took the time to explain to me about *Mardi Gras*. *Mardi Gras*, French for Fat Tuesday, is the day of the big community gumbo and celebration before Ash Wednesday, which begins the Lenten season. Since Lent is forty days of sacrifice and fasting for the Catholics, *Mardi Gras* is the last chance people have to indulge in food and good times until Easter Sunday. The *Courir de Mardi Gras* is the "run of the *Mardi Gras* revelers" in an attempt to collect ingredients and money for the community gumbo.

Today, *Mardi Gras,* is weeks of celebrations that include going to parades, creating costumes, attending balls, and catching beads; but in the decades of the early 20th century it served a practical purpose. Practical or not, I found it quite scary and surreal at age six. Besides, we didn't even attend the evening's entertainment. That was fine with me. I had had enough of *Mardi Gras* for one day, and I was sure Mom's gumbo tasted better anyway!

The Night the Music Died

It is way past bedtime, probably around one in the morning, and something wakes me up. My eyes open, and I see lights on in the kitchen. I hear my mom and sister whispering and muddling around. What's going on?

I get up hesitantly, still half asleep, walk out into the hallway and peek inside the kitchen. My mom and sister are distraught, but I can't figure out why.

"Why is everyone up?" I ask.

"Dad is sick," Mom replies. "He's in a lot of pain."

The door to their bedroom is open, and I look in. Dad, who has a ribbed undershirt and a sheet covering him to the waist, is hunched over on his side in bed. I can tell he is in great pain by the way he is curled up and by the pasty color on his face. I also see blood on the pillow and on the towel he is clutching. Now, I'm fully awake and frightened.

In order to call an ambulance, my sister is sent a quarter-mile down the road to the nearest neighbor who has a phone. She returns in about 20 minutes, saying the ambulance has been called and is on its way. On its way --but which way--we live way out in the country. There are many turns down dark gravel roads, some with no street signs, and there are several different ways to get here. How will they get directions if they get lost? How will they know which road to take?

It's a good thirty minutes' drive from the nearest town, and this ambulance is coming from Lafayette, even farther away. All these thoughts are running through my head but there is nothing I can do. I'm only ten.

We wait and wait! Mom tries to get Dad as comfortable as possible, but he is not moving or talking. On one of her trips through the kitchen, she urges me to go give Dad a kiss, and tell him goodbye. I shake my head no. I don't understand why I have to tell him goodbye. I'll see him in the morning. I'm rooted to my spot. I can't make myself go into the bedroom.

The ambulance finally arrives! With the efficiency, courtesy, and expertise of 1961 paramedics, they place Dad on a gurney, lift him in the ambulance-- which Mom also gets into--and take off to the hospital. I hope the trip back is much quicker than the trip here, I think.

It's almost dawn by this time. My sister and I get a few hours rest, and then my cousins arrive to pick us up, supposedly to go to the hospital. We detour to my married sister's house and it is there, while we are together as a family, they give us the news that Dad did not make it. He had suffered a heart attack. My dad is gone at the young age of fifty!

"Oh Dad, I'm so sorry. I wanted to give you a hug and kiss. I wanted to say goodbye. I thought I'd have time to do it. I give it now, Dad, along with all the other times I've given it in the last forty-seven years."

My dad never got to hear my goodbye, or feel my hug or kiss with his human body, but I know he's heard my voice and felt my embrace many times in his spirit body.

The wake is a two day and night affair, as they all are in our part of the state at the time. Family and friends take turns sitting at the funeral home, which remains open through the night. Food is brought in and people try to get Mom and me to go home and rest. Home--rest, two contradictions in terms for us.

On October 7, 1961, we bury Dad in the Richard cemetery, next to our Catholic church, near my school, and only three miles from our home. My entire sixth grade class is excused from school and allowed to walk the short distance to attend the funeral service.

The hurt, loneliness, and sadness are too difficult to write about and dwell on, but I can say that it went on for years. I had thought the first day of school was the end of my world as I knew it. I was wrong then, but I am not in error this time.

My childhood decade ends the day Dad dies, October 5, 1961, only five days before his 51st birthday, eight days before my 11th birthday and five weeks before his twenty-three year old daughter's wedding. That is the date I mark as the end of my first decade, and the end of life as I knew it. My world did a 180 degree turn. Things are very different in our home now. But that's another story and a different decade.

Afterword

There is a gift more precious than any financial inheritance, land holdings, and expensive jewels that we can bequeath to the next generation. That is the gift of culture, heritage, and family rituals. These are the treasures that give a family a sense of community, belonging, and commitment. The unique culture of Southwest Louisiana, which includes its music, food, language, and rituals, is deeply rooted in the hearts and souls of the Acadians, no matter where they may call home. It's what keeps them grounded in tradition and gives them a sense of continuity. Hopefully, that heritage and culture will not be lost on our life's journey through this new and fast paced millennium.

Acknowledgments

Special thanks to my husband, Glenn Bogan, for his support, encouragement, and patience during my writing phase and to my daughter, Michelle Honeycutt, who has always offered praise and encouragement for all my creative endeavors.

A big thank you to Sandy LaBry for planting the writing seed and for her editorial assistance.

Thank you to my siblings who offered forgotten details and shared their own memories and to my friends who listened, laughed, offered suggestions, and showed appreciation for my childhood recollections.

Biography

Yvonne Thibodeaux Bogan grew up in the rural farming community of Richard in Southwest Louisiana, an area also known to the locals as *la Pointe Noire*. She is a descendent of the exiled French Acadians originally deported from Nova Scotia in 1755. She grew up in a French-speaking family in an area inhabited mostly by other French-speaking Acadians with a passion for God, family, and tradition. Yvonne is a retired elementary school teacher currently living in Lafayette, Louisiana with her husband. Her hobbies include, painting, reading, tutoring, and writing.